D1610947

THE DESIGNER'S GUIDE TO JAPANESE
PATTERNS

JEANNE ALLEN

THAMES AND HUDSON

■ CONTENTS

First published in Great Britain in 1988 by
Thames and Hudson Ltd, London

First published in the United States 1988 by
Chronicle Books

Nihon Monyo Jiten by Takashi Katano was first published in Japan by Kawade Shobo Shinsha Publishers.

Edited by Terry Ryan
Cover design by Karen Pike
Translation by Barbarine Rich

Printed in Japan

■ INTRODUCTION

In 1972, a friend gave me a book of textile patterns that she thought might be an inspiration for my own work in print design. I loved the book for its bright beauty and original color combinations. Although the text was in Japanese, I assumed from the wide variety of design styles and the uniqueness of the motifs that the book was compiled from international sources.

Later that year, I made my first trip to the Orient and, like most visitors, was enchanted with the Japanese experience. I was particularly pleased to see the abundant evidence that the traditional arts were alive and flourishing wherever I went. Twenty-odd trips to Japan later, I realize that my introduction to the country was not entirely reflective of reality, and that, although old and new might sit side by side, my JAL calendar version of Japan is becoming harder by the minute to ferret out.

Much to my delight during that first visit, however, I began to spot designs from my favorite book, not as museum prints or in a priceless *Noh* theater robe, but in everyday things used in everyday life in Japan. At train stations, I found boxes of sweets wrapped in papers sprinkled with multi-colored fans, spinning tops, gaudy peonies, and tidy geometrics. Throwing away the cakes, I instantly became a collector of the wrappings. Near the same stations, I found small, intimate shops selling tiny lunch boxes, fat coin purses, folded paper dolls, and an endless assortment of personal vanities made from brightly colored textiles

and decorated papers. When I began to see the same patterns in kimono and *obi*, I realized fully that these design motifs were an intrinsic part of the culture and pervaded all aspects of Japanese life.

Since I could find nothing written in English on the history of these designs, I assumed that they were fairly modern graphics for the traditional arts turned out by talented studios, which are abundant in Japan. Only when I began working on *Designer's Guide to Japanese Patterns* did I realize that although many of the designs had been reinterpreted and transformed through the years, most of the patterns had antecedents going back more than nine hundred years to the Heian period (794–1185).

It is a popular belief that the Japanese are copiers, not creators. This book is testimony that nothing could be further from the truth. In the nine hundred years between the middle of the Heian period and the beginning of the Meiji period (1868–1912), there was a continuous outpouring of original work in literature, arts, and crafts. The first cultural inspirations in Heian times did come from abroad—mainly from China and Korea in the T'ang dynasty (618–907)—but by the eleventh century, the Japanese had absorbed the foreign influences and were displaying original expression in all their arts.

Chinese poetry, much favored by the court in the Nara period (710–794), had developed into the indigenous *waka* poetry. Simultaneously, in writing and calligraphy, the adopted Chinese characters were given a new set of purely Japanese sounds, which were documented in a formal *kana* syllabary. In the arts, *karakami* (Chinese decorated papers) evolved into *ryōshi* (Japanese decorated papers), and designs depicting Japanese subjects emerged. As the society developed and entered the Kamakura period (1185–1338), the culture became more recognizably Japanese. The military (samurai) class rose to power and began to develop its own patterns, which were characterized by their simplicity and subtle colorings (see examples 28 and 62) and were used primarily to decorate armor and leather military implements. The samurai avoided the intricate, exotic Heian designs because they were not appropriate for battle. At the same time, the designs that had originally appeared in the Heian court became the exclusive property of the Kamakura elite. These *yūsoku* patterns were much treasured by the aristocracy.

Even into the Edo period (1603–1868), certain patterns and designs were restricted to certain classes, and within these classes to certain families. With the rise of the merchant middle class in the Edo period, however, many of the old restrictions were broken down. The Edo period was generally a freer society, both socially and artistically. Instead of adhering strictly to a courtly version of a design, for example, Edo artisans preferred to create a less rigid interpretation —example 12 (Waves from the Blue Ocean) is a Heian original; example 13 (Waves from the Blue Ocean with Caps) is the Edo reinterpretation of that original. New versions of old designs resulted in a great burst of creativity, spurred on by the Rimpa School artists, who spearheaded the revival of classical Heian arts.

Creativity was encouraged further by new production methods, such as woodblock printing in 1760, which allowed the commercially minded Edoite printer to produce designs en masse for the first time. Although stencil prints were still an important art form, new designs that captured moments and moods from everyday Edo life became popular, along with block printing. The important artists of the period—Hiroshige, Toyokuni, Eisen, and Kuniyoshi—became famous for their *ukiyo-e* woodblock prints and paintings of Edo life. The same artists also designed a frankly commercial product known as *chiyogami* (rectangular woodblock-printed paper), which was purchased, not to be collected, but to be used in *origami*, in the making of intricate *ane-sama* (elder sister) dolls and folded envelopes, and as coverings for small boxes and books. These papers enjoyed an enormous market, and the demand for new designs and revivals of old traditional designs inspired a new burst of creativity. Designs from the twelfth century flourished again in the eighteenth century with a broader audience, and these once-restricted designs became a part of everyday life— that visual referent that westerners recognize as "Japaneseness."

Despite the westernization of Japan,

which began with the Meiji period and continues today, the Confucianist aspect of the culture teaches respect for ancestors and their ways, thereby protecting the life of traditional arts and crafts.

About This Book

Although not arranged chronologically, the 136 illustrated patterns shown in this book collectively mirror the country's political, cultural, and artistic history. Each of the six categories contains examples from the major historical periods, beginning with the Chinese-inspired Heian designs and followed by militaristic motifs from the Kamakura period, dramatic and bold designs from the extravagant Momoyama period (1576–1603), witty and original patterns from the inventive Edo period, and European-influenced patterns from the Meiji period.

A concise explanation of the way each design fits into Japan's cultural history accompanies each example. For practical purposes, the designs have been drawn to emphasize the personality of the motifs without regard to the medium in which they originated, so intricate weaving patterns and designs taken from rounded ceramic surfaces have been simplified and presented in styles that accentuate the timelessness of the graphics.

1 ■ *Inkin Karakusa* (Scrolling Vine Pattern Applied with Stamped Gold)

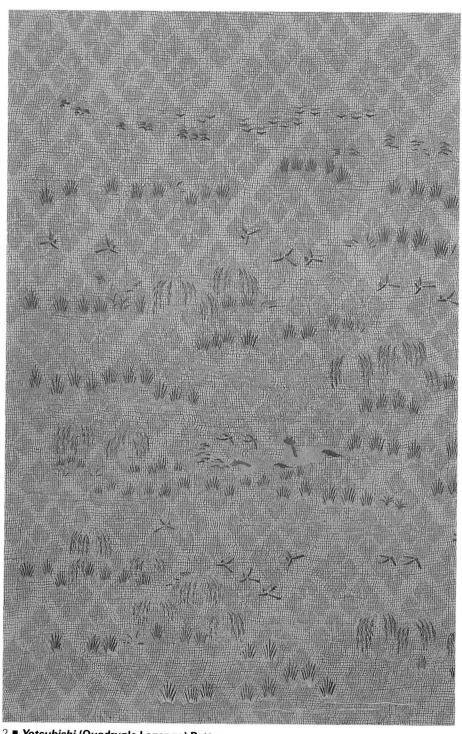

2 ■ *Yotsubishi* (Quadruple Lozenge) Pattern

3 ■ *Suhama* (Stylized Sandbar) Design

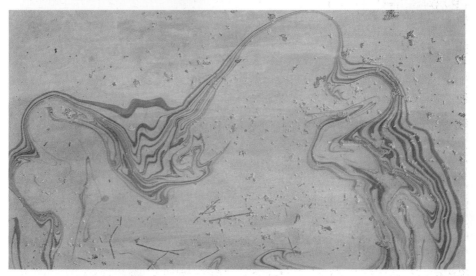

4 ■ Flowing Ink (Marbling) Pattern

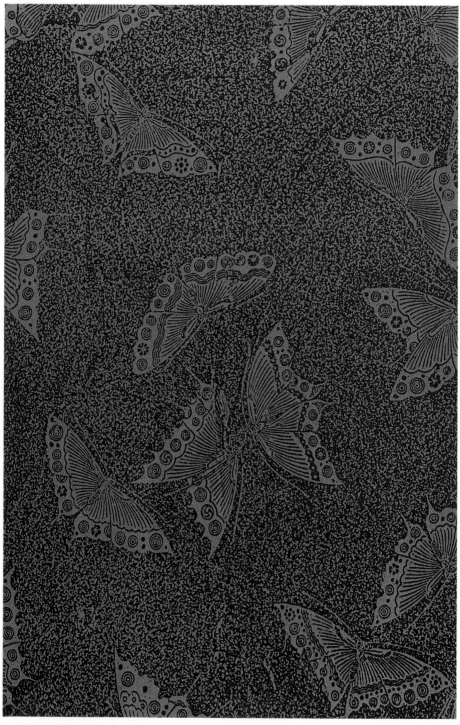

5 ■ Butterflies with *Nashiji*

6 ■ **Autumn Grasses and Deer**

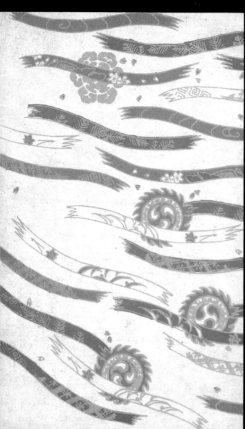

7 ■ *Noshi* (Auspicious Symbols) and Drums

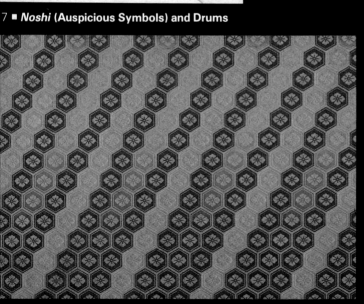

8 ■ Tortoise Shell and Flower Lozenge Pattern

9 ■ **Four Decorated Papers from Kyoto (*Ebōsho*)**

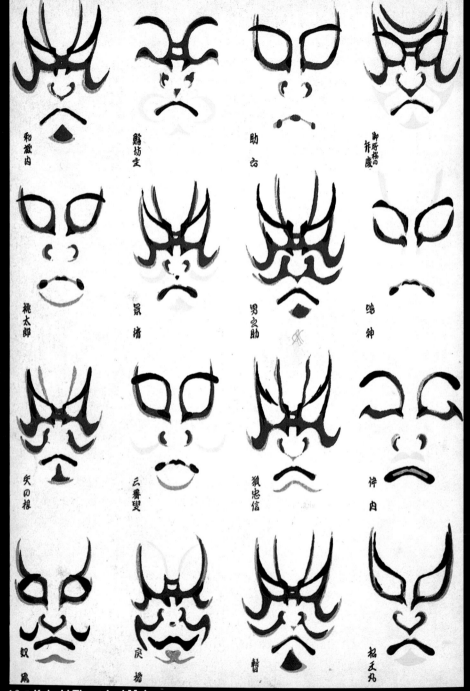

Designs from Nature

12 ■ *Seigaiha* (Waves from the Blue Ocean)

This orderly *seigaiha* pattern was first used in the Momoyama period (1576–1603) to decorate the sumptuous robes of the *Noh* theater. Initially applied in opulent gold leaf, the design became popular during the Edo period (1603–1868) in a miniature version used for kimono by the samurai class. Many variations of this pattern are used today, particularly for *chiyogami* and *ebōsho* (decorated papers). Although this interpretation may seem rather basic, the simplicity and elegance of the design have always been greatly valued.

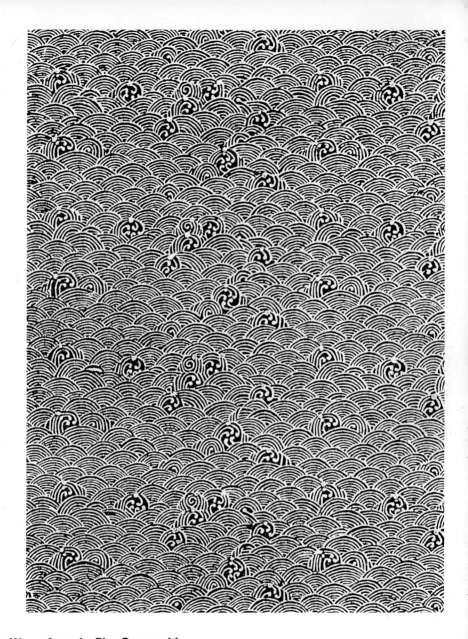

13 ■ Waves from the Blue Ocean with Caps

Although this free-spirited version of the wave motif shares the same *seigaiha* origin as the pattern on the previous page, similarities between the two end there. The first pattern was used almost exclusively by the elite classes, who valued the elegance and simplicity of the design. The easy, casual style of this second pattern, by contrast, made it appropriate for everyday use. Easily accessible, this version of the wave pattern became popular during the Edo period and remains in wide use today.

14 ■ Waves

A refined and elegant expression of the *seigaiha* motif, this design first gained importance as the background of the *Anthology of the 36 Poets*, famous poetry papers created in the Heian period (794–1185). The skillful execution of this wave pattern shows that the Japanese had fully absorbed the techniques seen in *karakami* (decorated papers), which had been imported from China. In later years, this small wave pattern was often used as a weave design for silk and damask.

15 ■ Flowing Water

This marbled design represents a technique, using ink, that originated in the Heian period. Highly prized for their exquisite line and delicacy, the Heian marbling techniques were lost during the long period of warfare that destroyed the tranquility of Japanese court life. Marbling was revived during the Edo period, but the fineness of the early work was never again duplicated. Edo artisans used carved woodblocks for a marbled effect, thereby sacrificing much of the fluidity of the design.

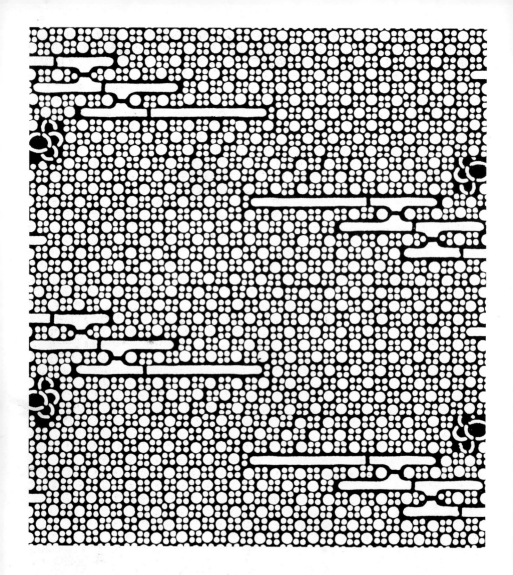

16 ■ Hail and Water Drops

Abstract designs, such as this one, usually began as recognizable representational compositions. These patterns gradually became more abstract through the subtle variations and simplifications introduced by artists over a long period of time. Abstraction of designs acceler- ated during the Edo period, when patterns previously reserved for the exclusive use of the aristocratic and warrior classes became accessible to the townspeople, who were gaining political power.

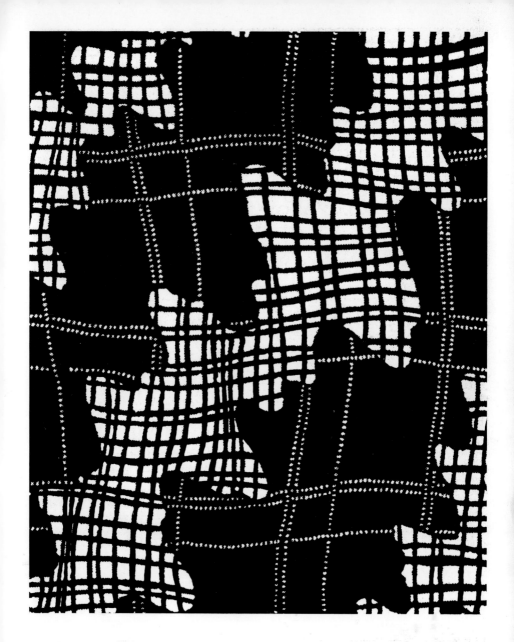

17 ■ Puddles and Lattices

Japanese court designs of the Heian period were noted for their formality and rigidity. Artisans of the Edo period, however—heady with the potential freedoms of a new age—produced fresh new interpretations of traditional designs. Although the original pattern for this design was based on straight lines, artists radically transforrned the results by pulling the cloth during the dyeing process. The puddle shapes are still recognizable, but the floating lattices give the design a modern, fresh look.

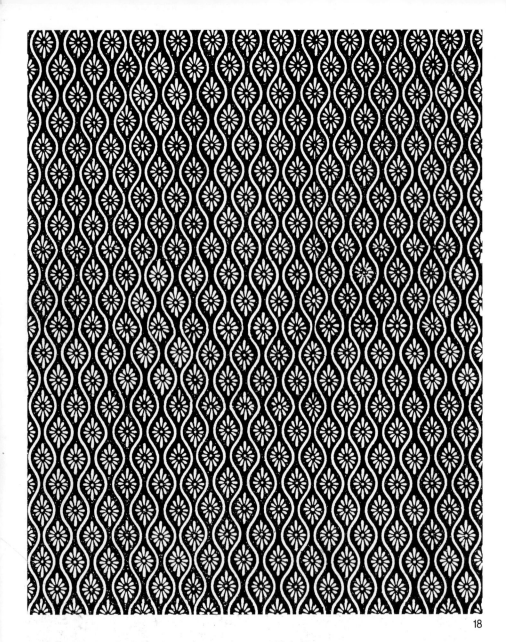

18 ■ Undulating Clouds

A common pattern used in clothing and military decorations of the ancient court, this undulating cloud (*kumotatewaku*) design is said to have originated from an image of "rising steam." Subsequent abstractions created the stylized floral form you see here.

19 ■ Flames

One of the oldest Japanese designs, this religious pattern often appears on ceremonial drums or on halos behind Buddhist statues. Exemplifying the magnificence of Buddha, this ritualistic design would never be used in a commonplace way.

20 ■ Moon and Autumn Grasses
This startlingly beautiful image of a large autumn moon surrounded by tall grasses was first used in military coats worn over armor. Adapted by the Rimpa School artists of the Edo period, the design remains influential today.

21 ■ Moon and Pampas Grasses
Another design revived and reinterpreted by the Rimpa artists, this original Heian design still looks strikingly modern. The waning moon here is sophisticated and poetic, and the design is still a popular image for summer and early fall textiles.

25 ■ Imaginary Buddhist Flowers

Many flower and vine patterns in this section show a pronounced Indian influence because they developed as a part of Buddhism. The designs accompanied the religion to China, then to Korea and Japan. This particular type of design is known as *bussōge*, an imaginary Bud-dhist floral pattern. The *bussōge*, which resembles the hibiscus, was an extremely popular decorative motif in China and Japan that mysteriously disappeared from use shortly after the Heian period.

26 ■ Honeysuckle

This delightful honeysuckle pattern is part of a rich cultural heritage that can be traced back to paintings in Korean tombs and Chinese caves. The honeysuckle flower, with its sweet nectar, has always stirred the imagination of artists in the East and the West. In Japanese art, this motif can be found as early as the Asuka period (552–710), where it appears on the halos of the Hōryūji Temple's Buddha Triad and on the pedestals of the Four Guardian Kings.

27 ▪ Thistle

Scroll vine patterns like those shown in examples 24–27 are extremely versatile designs. For one thing, the variations possible through combining and recombining the motifs are almost infinite. Also, although these compositions appear to have physical limits, each has a con- tinuity that would allow the pattern to go on endlessly on a larger area. The integrity of this thistle pattern, for example, would be maintained in spite of changes to the design's motif or size.

28 ▪ Ferns

This stunning pattern of two intersecting mountain ferns seems strikingly modern because of its simple graphic character. Actually, the design was created in the Kamakura period (1185–1338) to decorate and camouflage military clothing and arms. Usually stenciled on helmets and body armor in black, brown, or green, the design had a quiet, subdued quality, in contrast to the bold and colorful designs that were popular in peaceful circles but dangerous on the battlefield.

29 ■ Reeds

Like the previous design, this small, clean pattern showing reeds growing in water was used in the Kamakura period to adorn military armor. All of these camouflage patterns were applied by using a *kusube* stencil technique. From its military heritage, this reed design then became popular in the decoration of the samurai kimono and, eventually, for working clothes worn by farmers. In this example, the rows are slightly askew, creating the impression that the image is reflected on water.

30 ■ Sea Moss

This elegant, ancient design depicts a seaweed that grows on rocks in shallow ocean water. As in the design, the branches of the moss grow out in an almost perfect circle. In the early Heian version of the motif, each ball of sea moss was arranged independently; this overlapping, linear arrangement came later during the Edo period. The simple strength of the design has clearly withstood the usual temptation to change the original image in any way other than the placement of the motif.

31 ■ Flower Diamonds

Few Japanese designs are composed of a single motif, making this flower diamond pattern a rarity. Designed in the Heian period and used exclusively in that time by the ancient court, the motif became a powerful social symbol— much like the Louis Vuitton pattern of today. In modern times, this consistently popular pattern is freely used in everyday ways by everyday people—an inconceivable idea in ancient times.

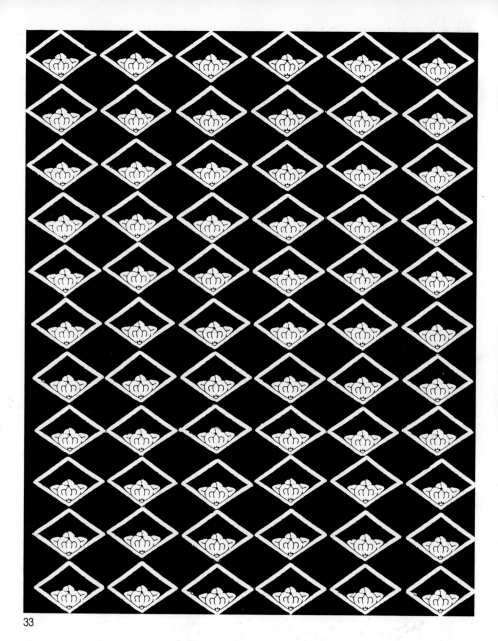

33

32 ■ Lotus Leaves and Water Plants
This delicate design emerged from the Edo period as a pattern used in the cotton summer kimono (*yukata*). The fine-lined patterning shows the artist's effort to create a cool, refreshing image for the heavy heat of Japanese summer.

33 ■ Mandarin Orange Flowers in a Diamond Crest Pattern
This motif is often used as a family crest by actors and the head families of traditional Japanese dancing schools. Originally used in court clothing and interior decoration, the motif has remained a private and very exclusive symbol.

34

35

34 ■ Hemp Leaves
Originally, this pattern was most popularly used to decorate the clothing of newborn babies. Hemp grows so quickly that parents used the design in the hope that the plant's vigor would be transmitted to the infant.

35 ■ Japanese Plums
This simple face-on view of an open plum blossom is famous as the crest of Tenjin Sama, the god of learning. Using a single motif, this plum design draws its energy and appeal from its simplicity.

36

36 ■ The Four Graces

This design represents the four seasons—also called The Four Graces. The combined images of orchid, plum, bamboo, and chrysanthemum also hint at the traditional Chinese themes of the four graceful arts: calligraphy, *koto* (lute playing), chess, and painting.

37 ■ Bamboo Leaves

This simple, sophisticated design showing bamboo leaves in a vertical fall skillfully uses dark and light to create the illusion of density and void. The artist worked within the width limitations of the kimono *obi*, which is very narrow.

41 ■ Irises and Rock-Filled Embankment Baskets

The image of irises blooming in rushing river water is a visual summer poem. The pattern has charm, despite the less-than-skillful brushwork of the artist. The careful placement of the images recalls the Edo period colloquialism "Space has not been pulled out." That is, the composition retains a flat, primitive character. As contemporary artists have proven, the success of a composition does not depend solely on the skill or accuracy of its painting.

42 ■ Irises and Flowing Water

These irises, drawn much more realistically than those in the previous pattern, clearly lack the strength and personality of the others. Actually, the entire composition is lacking. The repetition of the images appears mechanical and flat. To make the pattern more inviting, the placement of the design should be less predictable, or other elements (a riverboat or a bridge) should be added. This design is made interesting only by trying to determine how it fails.

Animal Designs

44 ■ Flying Cranes

This motif originated with the Rimpa School during the Edo period. Highly influential in Japanese art, the Rimpa artists were responsible for a classical revival of the Heian period. The artists, following master Hon'ami Kōetsu (1558–1637), created a calligraphy and a style of illustration that reinterpreted Heian subject matter in an exciting and vital way. The dramatic and evocative cranes in this design, for example, seem to fly off the picture plane.

45 ■ Geese

Probably the most popular and enduring art movement of the Edo period was that of the *ukiyo-e* woodblock prints. Prints that illustrate *ukiyo* ("floating world") subject matter are known as *ukiyo-e*. Geisha, sake, and the world of theater were favorite subjects of such *ukiyo-e* artists as Andō Hiroshige (1797–1858), who was known for his landscapes. The geese in this pattern were probably modeled after geese in the style he made famous in woodblock prints of birds and flowers.

46

47

46 ■ Phoenixes, Birds, and Scrolling Vines

This early phoenix pattern, designed to decorate the reverse side of an octagonal mirror, clearly shows the Persian influence that came to Japan via China and Korea during the Asuka period.

47 ■ Paired Phoenixes

This piece is total fantasy—neither phoenixes nor flowers are real. The phoenix motif, however, was important in Heian culture, appearing often in designs and architecture, including the famous tenth-century Phoenix Hall near Kyoto.

48 ■ Horses and Stylized Irises

At first glance, this design featuring horses and irises might be mistaken for a stenciled pattern from eighteenth-century New England. The horses are shown galloping between what appear to be church steeples, complete with crosses. Actually, the design is definitely Japanese in origin and was created in the Kamakura period to decorate military armor. The design is still used for Boys' Day on the fifth of May each year in displays of ancient armor and warrior implements.

50

49 ■ Lions and Scrolling Vines
The lions in this military decoration
appear fearsome and threatening, and
the speckled area simulates sharkskin.
The total effect is one of combined
strength—the king of the land and the
king of the sea, the lion and the shark.

50 ■ Dragonflies
Unlike other animal motifs, the dragonfly
does not project an image of force. Perhaps this military decoration was
designed by an artist who doubted war's
glory. Perhaps the dragonflies represent
the first waves of warriors who were
inevitably killed.

52

51 ■ Bats
This whimsical Edo period pattern
depicting bats in evening flight is almost
abstract because of the simplicity of its
execution. Although deceptively simple,
this skillfully rendered design can be
either cut off or expanded limitlessly.

52 ■ Bats and Dots
This bat composition is far more complicated than the previous design because
the bats are massed together in an interlocking pattern. In a much larger design,
the bats would become abstract forms
linked together in a patchwork pattern.

54

53 ■ Thunder Gods
This design clearly shows how natural phenomena were perceived in early Japanese culture and how intensely the culture was involved with the turbulent elements. Images of thunder gods beating drums are also found in painting and sculpture of the period.

54 ■ Lions
Symbolizing the curl of the lion's mane, this pattern is worn in white on a dark green background by the lion dancer during festival time (*matsuri*). The dancer's fearsome image is heightened by the wearing of a red lacquer mask.

55 ■ Dragon Flames

Probably introduced during the Heian
period, this Chinese design represents a
dragon turning into flames in two interlocking circles. Unlike most designs of
Chinese origin, this motif has never been
altered and is still greatly admired for its
elegance.

56 ■ Dragon Waves from the Blue Ocean

Like the phoenix, the dragon is a mythi-
cal beast borrowed from Chinese lore
that was used extensively in military
clothing of the Kamakura period. The
image of power emanating from the fire-
breathing beast was probably more than
enough to impress an enemy.

56

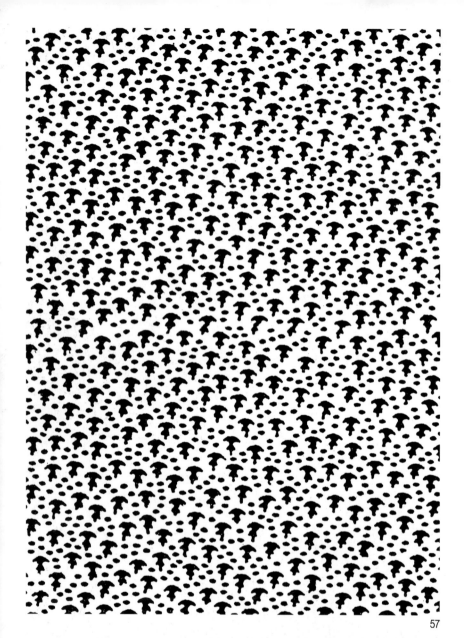

57 ■ Firefly Squid

Similar in layout to the bat patterns, this tiny repetitive design represents a kind of Japanese squid that glows in dark water. The bubbles surrounding this unusual sea creature give the pattern a sense of effervescence.

58 ■ Catch from the Sea

Although this highly stylized composition of lobsters, fish, and octopus seems very modern, it is at least as old as the Edo period. Second only to rice as an important food to the Japanese, sea creatures have always been a popular design motif in the culture.

59 ■ Sea Creatures

This intricate design was probably designed by Edo artisans, who were noted for their skillful stencil carving. Such delicate work only became possible when sophisticated stencil tools were formed in the Edo period. If the stenciling skill of that era is apparent, so is the wide range of subject matter. Edo art used everyday objects as design motifs. Common people and all that concerned them became a theme that had finally come into its own.

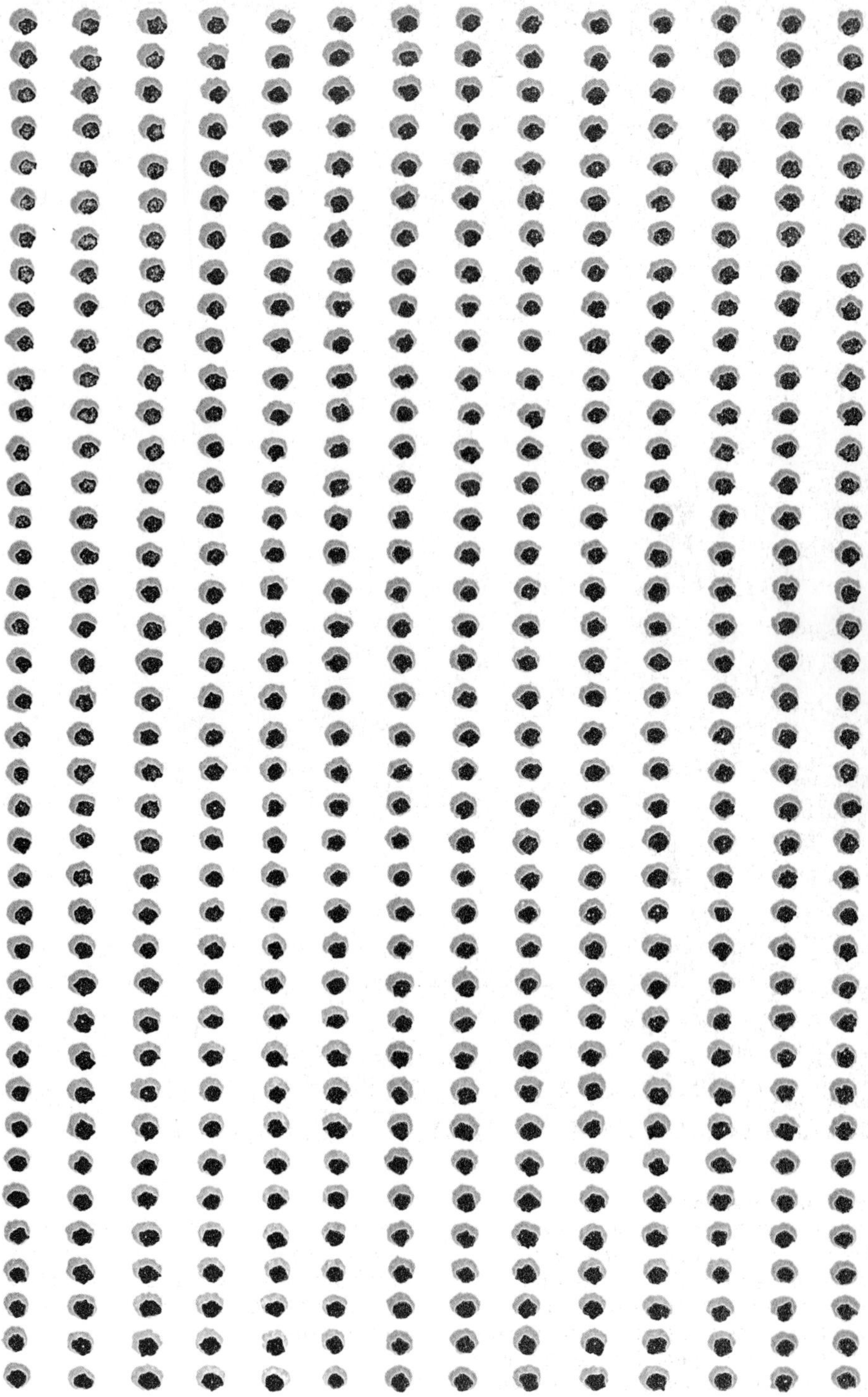

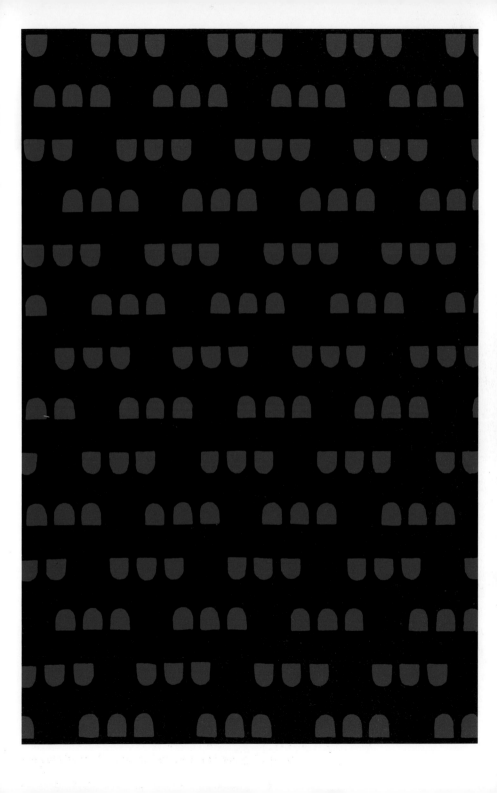

63 ■ Diagonal Hemp Leaf Pattern

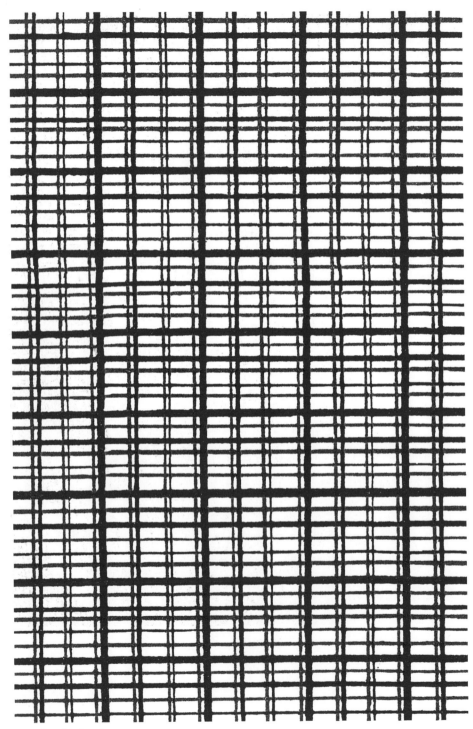

67 ■ Linked Miniature Patterns

Geometric Designs

69

70

71

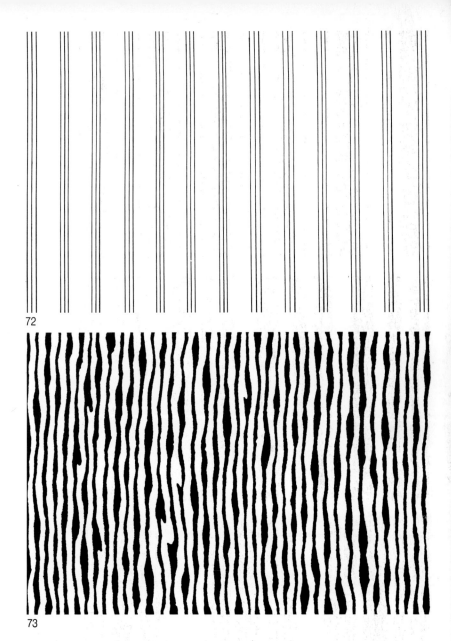

72

73

69–73 ■ Five Types of Stripes

An important fashion in the Edo period and known as *kando* (side road), each of these stripes had its own significance and history. The two-sided stripe in example 69 shows a thick stripe bounded by two thin ones. The stripes in example 70 become increasingly thicker, and the thick stripe in example 71 is surrounded by stripes that become increasingly thinner. The aristocratic-sounding *daimyō* stripes in example 72 were used in common, everyday ways. Example 73 was inspired by the irregularity of spun cotton pulled taut.

74

75

76

77

74–76 ■ **Three Types of Stripes**
The undulating lines in example 74 make the design look like modern op art. The Hakata stripe in example 75 was designed after a famous weaving pattern from the city of Hakata on Kyushu Island. Snakeskin patterns inspired the stripes in example 76.

77 ■ **Diagonal Stripes and a Balancing Acrobat Doll**
This playful stencil design from the Edo period reflects the popular culture of the time. Within the bold diagonal white stripe, carp swim upstream in a waterfall. The black stripe holds balanced toys.

78 ■ Diagonal Stripes with Flowers and Lightning

Decorative stripes like this one and the acrobat stripe on the previous page were considered very stylish during the Edo period. This series of seemingly unrelated motifs becomes a coherent design because of the thick and thin diagonal stripes that are repeated between the unrelated patterns of diamond-shaped chrysanthemums, squared chrysanthemums, peonies, and lightning zigzags.

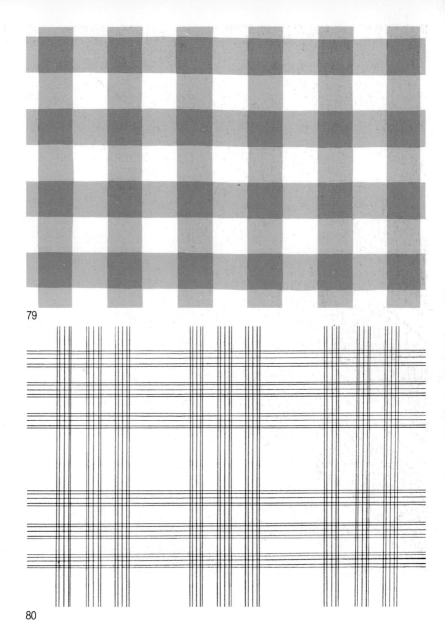

79

80

79 ■ *Benkei* **Plaid**
First made famous on stage as decoration for the costume of *Benkei,* the well-known Kabuki theater role, this popular pattern is characterized by lines that intersect both vertically and horizontally and is often made in bright, contrasting colors.

80 ■ **Three-Stripe Lattice**
The popularity of stripes, plaids, and lattices during the Edo period was due in part to advances made in weaving techniques during that time. New looming and dyeing technology, introduced from China, made innumerable design variations possible.

81

82

81 ■ *Koma Gōshi* (Small-Room) Plaid
The thin lattice lines in this plaid are placed between a thicker lattice to form the "small rooms" the pattern is named after. The thin and thick lattices are usually colored differently to contrast with the background color.

82 ■ Bean Paste Strainer Plaid
The unusual name for this design comes from an everyday utensil—made of woven horsetail and stretched across a circular box—that was used to strain bean paste. Mashed bean paste was pressed through this sieve with a wooden spatula.

83 ■ Checkers

This classical pattern reached its height of popularity during the Genroku era of the Edo period. First seen on the Kabuki stage in high contrasting colors, the checkers design later became a favorite pattern for both the kimono and the *obi* sash of the common people. The slightly irregular edge of each square gives the simple, clear design a woven look and adds a sophistication that would be missing if the squares were perfect.

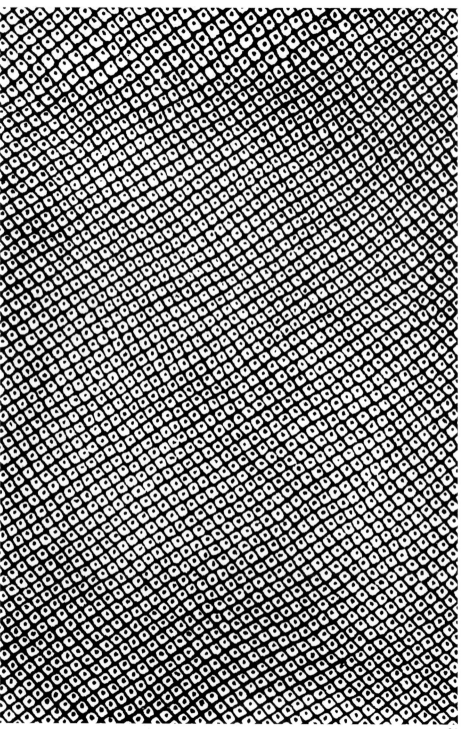

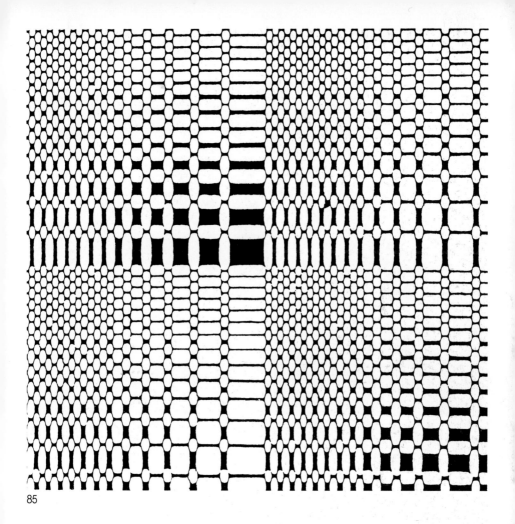

85

84 ■ **Spotted-Fawn Tie-Dye Pattern**
Although the art of tie-dyeing existed in
pre-Heian times, Edo artisans perfected
the techniques that produced work as
fine as this. This pattern was made by
tying silk cloth in different places and
immersing the whole piece in dye.

85 ■ **Varying Checkers**
Appearing absolutely modern, this pattern was probably designed in the Edo
period, when appreciation for graphic
geometric designs was at its height. The
design seems to be composed of two
sets of similar squares, but each set is
unique.

86

87

86 ■ *Shibaraku* Pattern
The striking graphic character of this design, in which wooden measuring boxes are stacked precariously on edge, made it especially suitable for the Kabuki stage. The design is large in scale and is usually stencil-dyed on the silk cloth.

87 ■ Joined Dice
In this Edo period design associated with dice playing and other games of chance, two vertical stripes separate a strand of black and white, positive and negative squares. High-spirited and witty, the pattern is still in widespread use today.

88 ■ Scales

This strong, uncomplicated pattern has the same graphic simplicity as the checkers design in example 83. The carefully composed rows of identical triangles in contrasting colors suggest the scales of a snake (hence, the title). An important symbol in theater, the design usually denotes a bewitching woman or a combative man. In the play *Dōjōji*, the main character sheds one kimono decorated with cherry blossoms to reveal her evil nature, as symbolized by the scales decorating a second kimono.

89 ■ Parent and Child Scales

This pattern is a variation of the previous motif, but here the triangles are clustered in large and small (parent and child) shapes. The design was probably invented by Chinese artists for the weaving of semi-precious silk brocades, known as *meibutsu gire,* brought to Japan through the southern Asia trade route. Highly prized in both China and Japan, the most treasured pieces of *meibutsu gire* were woven with threads of gold leaf.

90 ▪ **Tortoise Shells**

Composed of interlocking hexagons, this design acquired its name because of the obvious similarity between the motif and the markings of the tortoise. There are many variations on this pattern, which was originally the exclusive property of the samurai class. This particular version is the most basic interpretation and became very popular during the Edo period, when it was widely used as a kimono pattern for the working class.

91 ■ Tortoise Shells and Turtles

In Japan, the turtle is highly prized as a design image and as a food that imparts virility and good health to those lucky or rich enough to eat it. Although this delightful, whimsical example has an almost childlike feeling, the design was used only on decorated poetry papers in the Heian court by the most elite members of the nobility. The design eventually disappeared because its use had become so exclusive that artists lost the ability to reproduce it.

92 ▪ Tortoise Shells and Cranes

The citizens of Tokyo during the Edo period were known for their iconoclastic chic. They delighted in making common use of images and patterns that had been previously reserved for the exclusive use of the elite classes. This design, for example, showing the two auspicious symbols of long life—the turtle and the crane—showed a level of disrespect for the samurai class (whom the Edo middle class loved to taunt) by using their sacred symbols in a casual way.

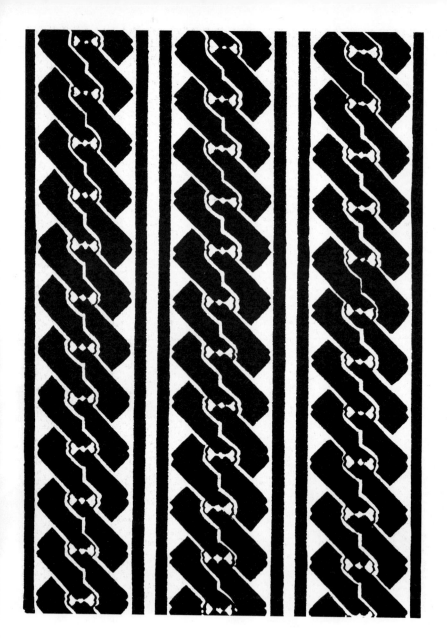

93 ■ Yoshiwara Links

During the Edo period, the Yoshiwara district of Tokyo was known as a pleasure quarter—the site of geisha houses, drinking establishments, and gambling rooms. This pattern was first worn in Yoshiwara and can be easily identified in the *ukiyo-e* woodblock prints of the period. A famous painting from the Meiji period (1868–1912) shows a geisha wearing this pattern in a jacket and a head covering; she also carries a lantern encircled by these Yoshiwara links.

94 ■ *Saya* **Pattern**

This pattern has a distinctively Chinese personality and did, in fact, originate in China as a woven textile. First brought to Japan in Heian times, the design did not become popular until the Edo period, when it was redesigned as a stencil pattern. At first glance, the pattern appears to be complicated, but it is actually a simply constructed series of links. This interesting, durable design is still highly appreciated and often used on satin and damask.

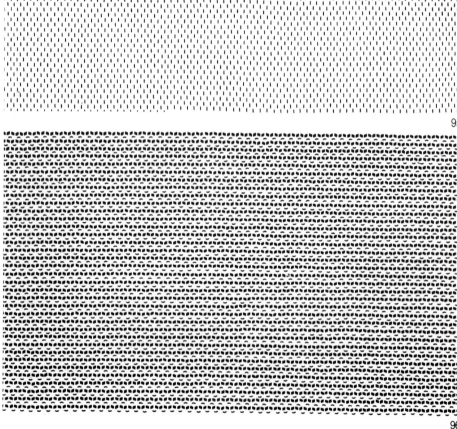

95

96

95–100 ■ Six *Komon* (Minute Patterns)

These Edo period designs were highly
valued because of the skill required to
cut the stencil into such small patterns.
To prepare the stencil paper (*washi*), the
artist first coated the paper with persimmon juice for strengthening, laid it on a
board, dried it with bean paste, and
carved out ten layers at a time.

Example 95 imitates *ikat* or *kasuri*
dyeing, in which the fiber is dyed in
selected areas to create special effects
when the material is woven. The *kobako*
(small-box) pattern in example 96 was
used exclusively for decorating samurai
clothing. In the finest examples of this

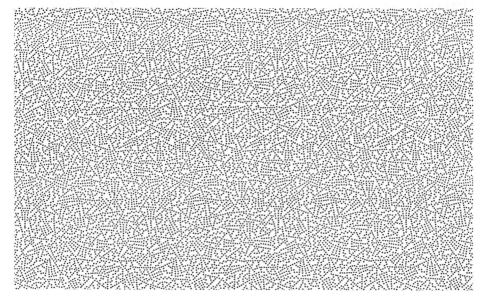

97

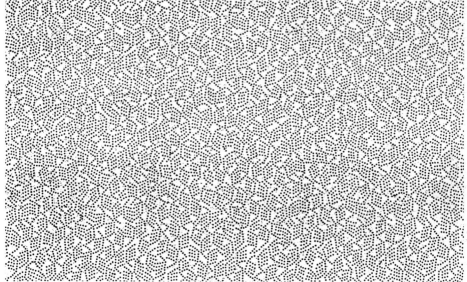

98

design, even the minuscule corners of the boxes are visible. Example 97, with its open and half-open fans, is one of the most delicate and skillfully executed of these minute patterns. The roof tiles in example 98 were carved with the same type of knife used to carve the fan pattern.

In the sharkskin pattern in example 99, the unsteady dots may have been carved by an amateur. The scattered cherry blossoms in example 100, on the other hand, have been skillfully punched out with a round chisel.

99

100

Domestic Designs

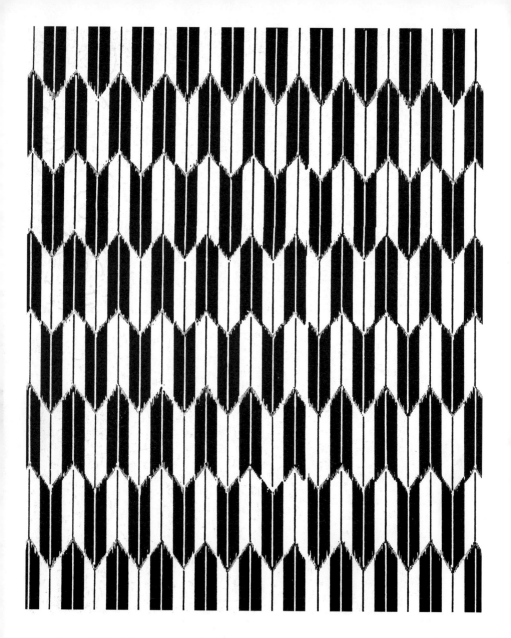

102 ■ **Arrow** *Kasuri*
This pattern, which was introduced in the Edo period, is a good example of the then-popular fashion to use everyday objects as subjects for art and design. Unlike Heian period patterns, which were reserved for very specific occasions, Edo patterns were used freely. Progress not-withstanding, this design was used commonly for servants' kimono patterns in the homes of noblemen. Since the Meiji period, it has also been used in students' graduation gowns.

103

104

103 ■ Arrow Wheels

On Boys' Day each year, brightly colored kites in the shape of carp are flown over Japanese houses. To add to the festive atmosphere, a wind wheel is placed at the top of the carp kite. This design is also used in summer kimono patterns.

104 ■ Imperial Cart Wheels

The ox cart, because it was the sole property of the aristocracy at one time, has a special significance in Japanese history. Although its origins may be archaic, the ox cart wheel as a design motif in this pattern is fresh and modern.

105 ■ Hearing-Good-Things Pattern

Typical of Edo wit, this pattern is a riddle with an auspicious message. The first object, an ax, translates as "good." The second object is *koto* (a stringed instrument), which is a homonym for "something." The third object is *kiku* (a chrysanthemum flower), which is a homonym for the verb "hear." Although inappropriate for everyday wear, this pattern has always been used for happy coats and for *noren*, the small curtains advertising that Japanese shops are open for business.

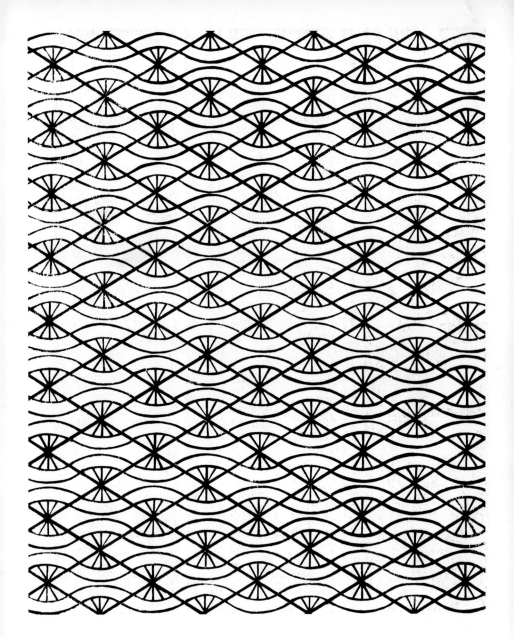

106 ■ Fans and Undulating Lines

Originating as an ancient court design, this pattern is not only beautiful but notable for its clever construction. The appearance of the design changes, depending on whether it is viewed from top to bottom or from side to side. The two fans placed at the intersections of the diagonal lines are continuously repeated, but the design is calculated so that the outline of each fan connects to another, forming an undulating line.

107 ■ *Bangasa* (Billboard Umbrellas)

This *bangasa* pattern is used popularly on the decorated papers (*chiyogami*) that cover small boxes and that are used to make brightly colored paper dolls. From the Edo period until just before the war, paper umbrellas like the ones depicted here were used to advertise the products of small merchants and innkeepers. Used both for sun and rain, these umbrellas were Japan's version of the logo T-shirts that everyone wears today.

108 ■ Drums with Comma Shapes

Comma shapes were often used to decorate the skins of drums used in Japanese ceremonies. The two motifs were commonly used together because the comma shape originally represented water from a spring, and the sound of a drum circles around and spreads out in air just as water does in a pool. Although the origins of this design motif are ancient and can be traced back to imperial court dances (*bugaku*), this pattern still decorates festival drums, jackets, and headbands.

109

110

109 ■ Linked Abacus Beads
Despite the modernization of Japan, the abacus is still the favored counting tool in schools and businesses. This pattern of abacus beads laid out as a continuing stripe is usually printed onto men's working clothes, *tenugui* towels, or *obi* sashes.

110 ■ Mud Wall
This dashing pattern is best known as the decorative marking used for firemen's coats. Like the previous pattern, this design was used almost exclusively by men, but in lighter colors and using larger shapes.

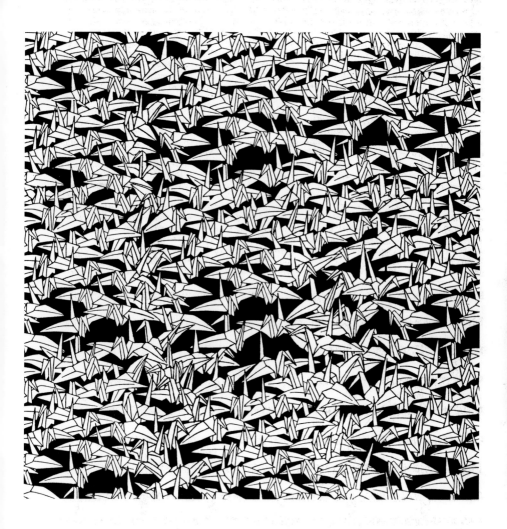

111 ■ Folded Paper Cranes

Origami (paper folding) originated in the Edo period and remains a popular activity that is an intrinsic part of the Japanese traditional arts. Although countless forms and shapes have been used in this art form, the most popular subject is the crane. Many different *origami* cranes have been designed throughout the years, including one with over one hundred wings and made from a single sheet of paper. Eventually, the design was transferred to cloth, as this example shows.

112 ■ *Ane-Sama* (Older Sister) Paper Dolls and Ohara Women

All young Japanese girls learn the traditional arts of the tea ceremony, flower arrangement (*ikebana*), kimono wearing, and doll making. Doll making combines the two arts of *chiyogami* (decorated paper) and *origami* (paper folding). The Ohara woman is easily recognizable from folklore as a woman carrying firewood from a country village outside of Kyoto. The *ane-sama* figure, although not so refined a character as the Ohara woman, has a tall, upright pose that is very attractive.

113 ■ *Uchiwa* (Round Fans)

It is still a common sight in Japan to see people strolling down the street on a warm summer evening dressed in *yukata* (summer kimono) and *geta* (wooden sandals) and fanning themselves with brightly decorated *uchiwa*. This delightful pattern, usually printed in indigo blue on white cotton, celebrates summer. The front side of the fan shows a pine bow with Mount Fuji in the background, the back side a latticed pattern—both refreshing summer images.

114 ■ Basket Weave

This design takes its imagery from a hexagonal basket weave known as *jakago* (embankment basket weave). As early as the Kamakura period in Japan, openwork baskets made with long thin strips of bamboo were filled with large stones and placed by the river banks to dam streams.

The idea of these baskets set in the flowing water became a popular romantic image in the Edo period, and the design appeared on scrolls, lacquer ware, and *chiyogami*.

115

116

115 ■ Auspicious Symbols

By the time of the Edo period, each of these ordinary-seeming objects had come to be considered a good luck symbol. Each motif was a design unto itself and was used to decorate papers (*chiyogami*) that were sold as symbols of good fortune.

116 ■ Paper Cutouts of Everyday Objects

In this collection of everyday objects from the Edo period, each of the cutout symbols has an outline, making the individual images seem a bit stiff. Even so, each motif has an interesting, accomplished design.

117 ■ Spool and Thread Pattern
This graphic checkerboard pattern probably originated as the family crest of a spinner or weaver. The two interlocking spools repeated on the black squares are usually wrapped with brightly colored threads, giving the design a strikingly modern look.

118 ■ Actors' Family Crests
A collection of family crests belonging to actors of the Kabuki theater, this bold Edo pattern was initially printed as souvenirs for Kabuki enthusiasts. Later, the design was used to decorate clothing, small personal objects, and *chiyogami*.

118

119 ■ Linked *Noshi*

Noshi, which originated as thin, folded strips of dried abalone wrapped in paper, are used as ornaments on auspicious occasions. They are shown here in a characteristic form developed in the Keicho era of the Edo period. Textile designers picked up this type of Keicho *noshi* and greatly enlarged it by painting the motif from one corner of the back of a kimono to the sleeve on the other side. This interpretation is an excellent example of a motif borrowed from a common object used in everyday life.

120 ■ It-Doesn't-Matter Pattern

This, like the hearing-good-things pattern in example 105, is an Edo riddle design. The three motifs used in this pattern—a sickle, a circle, and the Japanese character for *nu*—line up to read *kamawanu,* which translates as "it doesn't matter." The character of the

pattern, like its name, is rough and rakish. Originally used on clothing worn by the Edo "fast set," the design later worked itself into the everyday kimono patterns of the townspeople.

121

121 ▪ *Chayatsuji* Pattern
Through the skillful implementation of
stencil-dyeing techniques, this landscape
pattern, which probably originated as a
painting having depth and perspective,
has been transformed into a flat design
that remains clearly defined.

**122 ▪ *Goshodoki* (Hints from The
      Imperial Palace)**
This design, which uses scenery and
everyday objects from inside the Imperial
Palace, is the work of a skilled Edo stencil
maker. The detail evident in the imperial
carts, curtains, and other objects indi-
cates that the designer was equally
skilled.

108

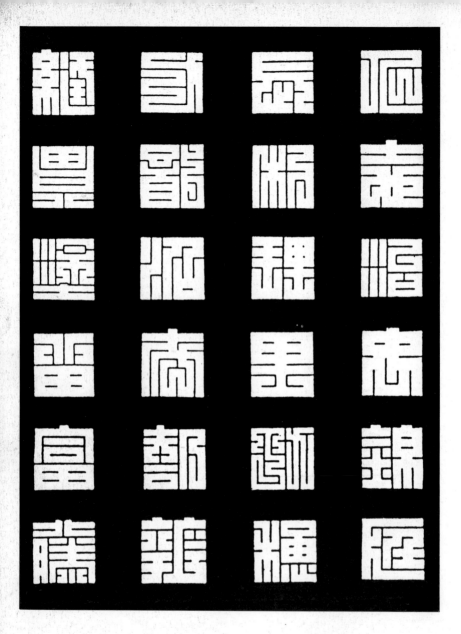

123 ■ Square Characters

During the Edo period, many distinctive styles of lettering (calligraphy) were designed for the popular entertainments, including drinking houses (*chaya*), sumo wrestling, and the theater. Few of these lettering styles have stood the test of time, one exception being this squarish, Chinese-inspired pattern. Originally designed to be used freely on garments and decorative objects, this simply shaped design retains its integrity no matter how many characters are lined up together.

Complex Designs

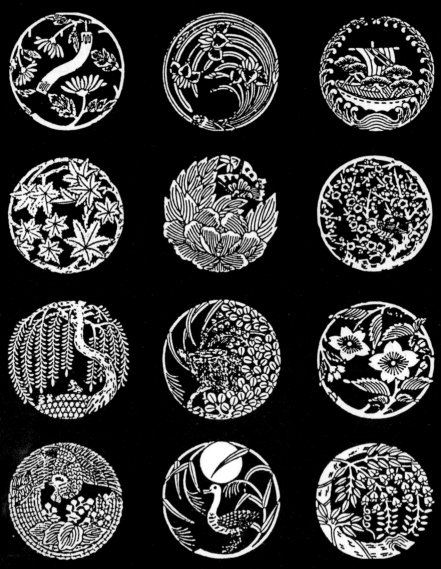

124 ■ *Hanafuda* (Flower Game) Motifs

125 ▪ Lion Hunting

Known also as the Hōryūji Temple Textile because it is preserved at the famous temple in Nara, this piece of brocade is a treasure imported to Japan during its early history. The fine weaving of this traditional design has never been duplicated. The magnificent composition of riders placed within a roundel and surrounded by *karakusa* (scrolling vine motifs) recalls the long, historic route such designs took in finally reaching Japan. Variations on this type of pattern can be found as far away as Europe.

126 ■ **Flowering Trees, Paired Phoenixes, and Paired Rams**

This Heian pattern, which is preserved at the Shosoin Treasure House in Nara, is the foundation for later scenic designs, such as the Edo period *chayatsuji* and *goshodoki* patterns in examples 121 and 122. In this design, heavenly creatures have been brought to earth and are shown together with birds and tropical trees. The sophistication of these sublime images is reminiscent of the richness and wisdom of Heian imagination.

127

127 ▪ Dragons in Double Roundels and *Karakusa* (Scrolling Vines)

Famous as one of the covers of the poetry papers known as the *Anthology of The 36 Poets,* this pattern was printed on ancient *karakami* brought from China to Korea and Japan. The famous anthology is now housed at Nishi Honganji Temple in Kyoto.

128 ▪ *Inkafu* (Cotton-Printed) Pattern

Inkafu designs, first produced in China for export, were carved into a wooden board and then printed onto a cotton ground cloth, a rare commodity in Japan then. This Edo reproduction uses the *katazome* (stencil with paste resist) technique.

128

129 ■ Autumn Grasses and Animals

This carved woodblock design of rabbits, dragonflies, and butterflies amidst bush-clover, bellflowers, pampas grass, maple leaves, and other autumn foliage is thought to be one of the oldest designs with native Japanese qualities. Executed on paper sized with lime and printed with mica, this design was inspired by *karakami* (papers imported from China). This design has an aristocratic character and is closely connected to the designs found in the *Anthology of the 36 Poets*.

130 ■ Stripes and Assorted Comma Shapes

One of the most popular Edo motifs for family crests was the comma shape. Dozens of variations were made on this simple design, many of which can be seen here, where an assortment of commas have been placed between stripes. Generally associated with the Edo culture, which valued textiles and decorative objects, the comma motif actually originated in Chinese and Korean art and later appeared in the Heian-period Japanese handscroll, *The Tale of Genji*.

131

132

131 ■ Flowers and Butterflies
This pattern exemplifies the kind of modern design that became popular with machine printing. The flowers and butterflies sprinkled across a white background, while pleasant to look at, do not compare with sophisticated Heian and imaginative Edo designs.

132 ■ Willows and Round Fans
This bold design of summer fans with butterfly tassles entwined with willow branches holds an important place in the history of *kosode* kimono. Despite the delicacy of line, the summer images are juxtaposed with skill and resolve.

119

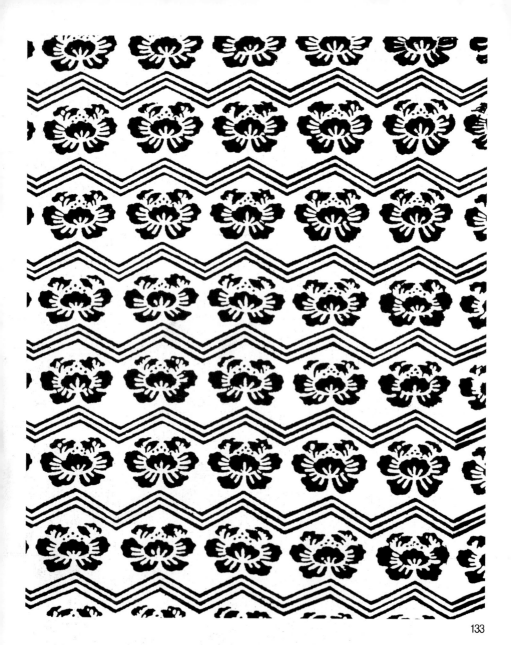

133

133 ■ Varying Stripes and Crab Peonies
Peonies or crabs? This delightful pattern
plays with our visual sensibilities until we
notice that the conventional peonies
separated by zigzagging lines have
become crabs. Now the design becomes
surreal and very interesting.

134 ■ *Kumo Shippō Tsunagi Tōka*
(Cloud of Linked Gems and
Wisteria) Pattern
This complicated stencil design, also
categorized as *komon* (minute patterns),
was created specifically for the narrow
width of the standard kimono cloth.

135

135 ■ Varying Pine Bark Diamonds
These intersecting diamond shapes are inspired by the irregular and rough surfaces of pine bark. In this version of the motif, the leveled diamonds are arranged at acute angles and decorated with tortoise shells, basket weave, scales, and water drops.

136 ■ *Bingata* Weeping Cherry Trees and Swallows
The *bingata* (crimson stencil dyeing) technique is particular to Okinawa, where mineral pigments are used to produce the bright clear-colored designs typical of the area. *Bingata* dyeing is famous for its open and informal patterns.

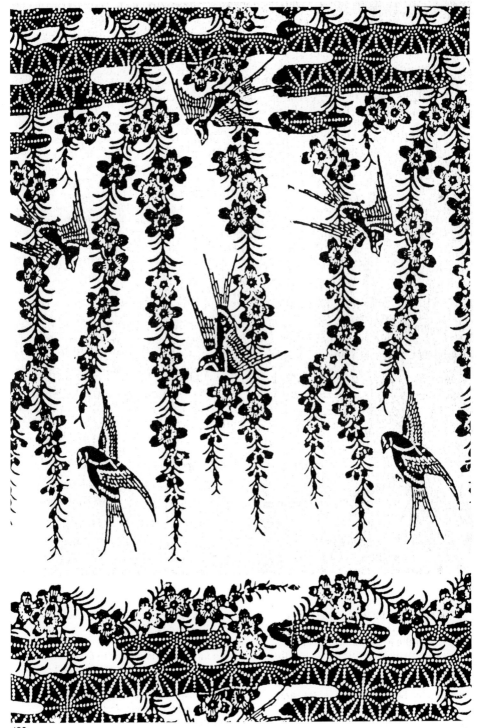

136

Descriptions of Color Plates

Pages 5 through 12

1 ■ *Inkin Karakusa* (Scrolling Vine Pattern Applied with Stamped Gold)
To create this rich, luxurious textile, the artist applies the pattern to colored cotton ground cloth with paste and then covers the entire piece with gold leaf. When the paste has dried, the extraneous leaf is carefully brushed away with a quill made from bird wings, leaving only the golden design.

2 ■ *Yotsubishi* (Quadruple Lozenge) Pattern
This landscape, which includes birds and horses, has been placed over a lozenge pattern, which is one of the most aristocratic patterns from the Heian period. The entire composition has been softened with a gauze-like haze.

3 ■ *Suhama* (Stylized Sandbar) Design
This stylized design, printed to look like a *sumi* (ink) seascape, is actually a carved woodblock pattern. The rock and pine tree motifs are printed in silhouette.

4 ■ Flowing Ink (Marbling) Pattern
Legend has it that the first marbled papers were created when *sumi* (ink) was poured into a small brook running near Nanzenji Temple in Kyoto and the pattern was captured on paper. In reality, marbling is achieved when a prepared ink is mixed in still water and paper is laid on top to catch the image.

5 ■ Butterflies with *Nashiji*
Nashiji, which translates literally as "pear ground," is the effect achieved by sprinkling gold dust over a lacquered background. The butterflies on this detail from a lacquer box were painted in relief.

6 ■ Autumn Grasses and Deer
In this autumn scene, the deer was tie-dyed onto a black ground and then a paste-resist was applied to achieve the design for the plants. To complete the lavish image, gold dust was sprinkled

over the ground and the entire design was embroidered.

7 ■ *Noshi* (Auspicious Symbols) and Drums
Although all the motifs in this design are ancient, the pattern itself is modern. Festive and bright, this popular design is often used today in *chiyogami*.

8 ■ Tortoise Shell and Flower Lozenge Pattern
Originally executed in gold leaf brocade *(kinran ori)* for *obi* and *Noh* theater robes, this diamond-shaped flower design has been placed within a tortoise shell grid. Dimension is created through gradation of color.

9 ■ Four Decorated Papers from Kyoto (*Ebōsho*)
In Japan's east (Tokyo), decorated paper is known as *chiyogami;* in the west (Kyoto), it is called *ebōsho*. The styles of the two patterns are as different as their names—the Tokyo patterns are simple and bright; the Kyoto patterns, rich and elaborate.

10 ■ Kabuki Theatrical Makeup
This delightful design illustrates how individual styles of makeup serve to identify the different actors in the Kabuki theater.

Pages 61 through 68

60 ■ Bean-Shaped Tie-Dye
Indicative of the Edo period, this tie-dye pattern was primarily used to decorate *tenugui* (narrow rectangles of printed cotton), which were then sewn together to make *hadajuban* (a garment worn under the kimono).

61 ■ Diagonal Lattice and Diamond-Shaped Flowers
Similar to examples 2 and 31, this design

Descriptions of Chapter Title Page Designs

uses diamond-shaped flowers within a green lattice.

62 ■ Leather Scales
This *kusube* stencil design is another example of a camouflage pattern that was probably created to decorate military armor and implements.

63 ■ Diagonal Hemp Leaf Pattern
Traditionally used for baby clothing, the hemp leaf pattern is usually colored pale blue, which is believed to bring good health. This particular pattern is a favorite choice for girls' clothing.

64 ■ Cherry Blossoms
The strength of this design lies in the surprisingly bold interpretation of the pattern. The artist has made the design very large in scale and ignored the fleeting, fragile qualities normally associated with cherry blossoms.

65 ■ Double Lattice
This double lattice design is an example of *iki* (Edo chic). The fashionable color combination is actually two grids of different colors—tea (green) and burnt tea (brown).

66 ■ Song Verses and Firemen's Standards
Casually interspersed on a background decorated with verses of song are *senjafuda*, cards once used for temple offerings. These particular cards are decorated with firemen's standards. This is a good example of an elegant and sophisticated design with a whimsical subject—typically Edo.

67 ■ Linked Miniature Patterns
This collection of miniature designs links together to form a kind of sampler or patchwork.

11 ■ Cloud and Snow Motifs
These motifs are derived from clouds and snow crystals. The third motif in the left row contains a Shinto paper offering, believed to represent a prayer for rain.

23 ■ Lattice and Chrysanthemum Balls
The centers of these circular shapes set within a grid contain motifs that resemble family crests.

43 ■ The Twelve Animals of the Zodiac
The twelve animals of the Zodiac, each within its own circle, originally were symbols used for direction and time.

68 ■ Zigzags and Four-Square Crests
These geometric motifs, consisting of triangles, hexagons, zigzags, and four-squares, were originally thought of as symbols of lightning. Their simplicity and directness make them seem very modern.

101 ■ Genji Incense Game Symbols
The Tale of Genji was a Heian-period novel about ancient court life. The Incense Game, using symbols based on the book, came later and was a popular pastime among the aristocracy.

124 ■ *Hanafuda* (Flower Game) Motifs
These motifs, also originating from a card game *(hanafuda)*, are arranged around floral motifs symbolizing the twelve months of the year. The game is played as part of the New Year's celebration.

■ GLOSSARY

Ane-sama Literally, elder-sister dolls. Elaborate, three-dimensional paper figures, usually with brightly colored hair ornaments and kimono, made of *chiyogami* (decorated papers). *Ane-sama* appeared in Japanese households as early as the late eighteenth century and have antecedents in continental Asia. Doll-making is a skill learned by all young Japanese girls.

Anthology of the 36 Poets A collection of poetry by 36 poets that was created to honor the Emperor Toba in 1112. Called *Sanjū Rokunin-Shū*, its 39 volumes were transcribed by twenty master calligraphers on decorated papers *(ryōshi)*. This work of art stayed in the imperial family until the sixteenth century, when it was given to the Nishi Hoganji Temple.

Asuka period Japanese historical era (552–710) tremendously influenced by the *Wei* and *Ch'i* culture from China. Buddhism was introduced to Japan in 530; Prince Shotuku (592–622) established laws that followed Buddhist thought and principles. The Hōryūji Temple in Nara was constructed in the Asuka period.

Bangasa Literally, billboard umbrellas. Paper-and-bamboo umbrellas suitable for sun or rain and used from the Edo period to the present as a means of advertising the products of small merchants, innkeepers, and other commercial enterprises. See example 107.

Boys' Day A national festival *(kodomo-no-hi)*, which is held on May 5th each year. In households and public buildings, adults display heroic objects and images (such as horses, irises, carp, and samurai armor and swords) in the hope that young boys will acquire the characteristics that the images symbolize. Each home flies two or three carp kites, for example, because the carp is respected for the power needed to swim upstream.

Bugaku Ancient imperial court dancing.

Bussōge An imaginary floral pattern, resembling hibiscus flowers, that is associated with Buddhism. Originating with the religion in India, the motif was brought first to China and Korea, then to Japan in the Heian period. The design entered Japan with imported papers *(karakami)* from China during its T'ang dynasty and is sometimes called the T'ang motif.

Chayatsuji Bleached hemp cloth dyed usually in indigo by means of the rice paste-resist method and used predominantly in landscape designs for *yukata* (summer kimono).

Chiyogami Rectangular papers decorated with printed patterns and considered to be auspicious. Originating in Kyoto, *chiyogami* became an Edo (pre-Tokyo) phenomenon that paralleled the popularity of *ukiyo-e*. Also used for doll-making and coverings for personal objects, *chiyogami* remains popular today.

Daimyō Provincial feudal lords.

Edo period Long, stable, and peaceful Japanese historical era (1603–1868). In 1590, military ruler Tokugawa Ieyasu centered his *bakafu* (tent headquarters) in the remote provincial center of Edo (present-day Tokyo). Eventually, the economic and cultural center of the country then shifted from Kyoto/Osaka to the Tokyo plain. The Edo period, which was free of influence from abroad because all foreigners were banned, was noted for its openness and creativity in society and the arts. Popular literature and art flourished in this time.

Ebōsho The decorated papers in Edo (Tokyo) that were known as *chiyogami* were called *ebōsho* in Kyoto, which was the earlier capital. *Ebōsho* patterns have a richer character than their bright *chiyogami* counterparts because of their muted colors, stenciling, and sophisticated motif combinations.

Hadajuban A kimono-like undergarment worn next to the skin; in summer, usually made out of bleached cotton or gauze for absorption.

Heian period Japanese historical era (794–1185) noted for its extraordinary concern for beauty, delicacy, and sensitivity in life and the arts. In 794, the imperial court moved from Nara to Heian Kyo (the capital of peace and tranquility), which was renamed Kyoto eleven centuries later. Under the strong emperors Kammu and Saga during the early part of the Heian period (794–897), Japan maintained active relations with T'ang China. Then, as the power of the emperors began to wane, one family of courtiers—the Fujiwaras—came to dominate affairs of state. After 894, communications with China were suspended, and the period from 897–1185 was called the late Heian, or Fujiwara, period. Japan then sought to develop its own artistic spirit. This shift of emphasis is clearly evident in the evolution of textile design and other arts.

Ikat A kind of predyed cotton cloth with patterns predetermined by the spacing sequences given the weft threads before weaving. The warp (lengthwise) threads are also dyed, and the expertise of the weaver brings the warp and weft threads together perfectly to create a two-dimensional design.

Iki Literally, chic. Referring to an Edo period stylishness based on savvy, not money.

Ikebana The art of flower arranging. One of the skills that Japanese women must learn to prepare themselves for marriage. There are many methods of *ikebana,* and many schools in Japan to teach the different methods.

Inkafu A printing technique, invented in China and exported during the Chou dynasty, wherein a design is first carved on a woodblock and then printed in indigo on cotton; also called *sai inkafu.*

Inkin Literally, stamped gold. A process in which gold leaf is directly applied or stamped onto the cloth. See example 1 and its description.

Jakago Literally, embankment basket weave. A kind of hexagonal weave of ancient origins used in Japanese basket weaving. See example 114.

Kabuki Japanese theater using dance, music, and mime in elaborately produced historical plays of moral conflict. Makeup and costumes are used symbolically to identify specific character traits. Considered the theater of the common people, Kabuki has been a popular art in Japan since the sixteenth century.

Kamakura period Japanese historical era (1185–1338) noted for its militaristic character. The artistically brilliant Heian period ended in 1185, when, after years of conflict, the Minamoto family defeated the rival Taira family and military families began their rise to power. Although the imperial court remained in Kyoto, its influence was lessened and Kamakura in eastern Japan was chosen as the seat of the shogunate. In the arts, the intricate and delicate Heian patterns gave way to the more practical camouflage patterns used to cover armor.

Karakami Elegant decorated paper originally imported from China to Japan during the Heian period. Also known as Chinese paper, it was made by covering select *torinoko* paper with *gofun* (lime) and printing the design in mica. Highly prized in ancient Japanese society, *karakami* provided the inspiration for the development of Japan's own cultural traditions.

Karakusa Literally, scrolling vine. A sequential pattern that is systematically organized so it can be endlessly expanded. An arabesque motif particularly characteristic of Heian patterns, *karakusa* can be traced from Persia to India, China, Korea, and finally Japan. See examples 24 and 125.

Kasuri See *Ikat.*

Katazome A printing method using a paste-resist and a stencil.

Kinran ori Literally, gold brocade. Silk threads wrapped in gold leaf woven in a brocade to produce an exquisite textile. Pieces of *ko kinran* (ancient gold brocade) have been preserved since Heian times and are highly prized for use in the Japanese tea ceremony.

Komon Miniature patterns carved into stencils and used in color dyeing. The patterns can be quite large, for some reason, and still be called *komon*. Artisans worked long and hard to design sharp, specialized blades to cut the intricate designs from paper layers strengthened with persimmon juice.

Kosode Kimono with relatively short sleeves. An everyday kimono that has been popular since the late Heian period. Worn also in *Noh* theater.

Kusube A dyeing technique used in the decoration of leather battle gear and leatherwear. The discovery of this technique allowed artisans to decorate leather armor with small, fine designs that became closely associated with the samurai class. See examples 29 and 62.

Meibutsu gire Ancient, semi-precious woven brocades from China brought by the southern trade routes and used to cover utensils for the tea ceremony. The most treasured pieces were woven in gold.

Meiji period Japanese historical era (1868–1912) in which Japan fully ended two centuries of self-isolation and welcomed contact with the West and its technological knowledge. By 1868, Emperor Meiji moved with his court from Kyoto to Tokyo, and a constitutional monarchy was formed. With the restoration of the monarchy, the country set out to master the science and technology that made western nations more economically strong. With the advent of this period, much of the early originality ended as Japan began to copy western dress, furniture, crafts, and art.

Momoyama period Japanese historical era (1576–1603) named after a castle built by unifying *daimyō* Toyotomi Hideyoshi. Hideyoshi stopped the building of temples and started the building of castles in Japan.

Nara period Japanese historical era (710–794) in which Japan was united for the first time. Named after the city of Nara, which is considered the ancient capital of Japan (Kyoto is the ancient capital). During this period, the Japanese were deeply influenced socially and artistically by Buddhism and T'ang dynasty China.

Noh Originally theater produced for the enjoyment of the ancient court. Kanze Kamome (1333–1384) established Noh as we recognize it today—drama, dancing, and mime accompanied by a chorus that chants the story in an archaic language. The pace of the drama is unbelievably slow and restrained. The gorgeous costumes are enhanced by the use of masks, which in themselves are treasures. The entire effect is heightened by the bleakness of the stage and the rigid formality of the play's movement.

Noren A short doorway curtain made of cloth used to signify that shops are open for business. Decorated either with a motif or with the shop's logo, these curtains are also used in homes for eye-level privacy.

Noshi Literally, a present. This term appears in *hiragana* syllabary as a decorative graphic or as a pattern of tied wrapping bands. Used on a gift to respectfully announce the presentation of the gift. In ancient times, the *noshi* was actually a strip of dried abalone, which was given as a gift on felicitous occasions. In present-day Japan, real dried abalone is only seen on the most expensive gifts. The custom, however, continues graphically—a printed image of the paper-wrapped strip of dried fish is attached to the gift. See example 119.

Obi A sash or cummerbund worn with a kimono. There are as many kinds of *obi* as there are fabrics, colors, and designs. The correct *obi* choice depends on the kimono, the season, the occasion, and whether the wearer is married or single. Often handwoven, the *obi* itself is a work of art.

Origami Literally, folded paper. This art form has its origins in the rituals of Shinto and Buddhist services, in which this folded paper was used to represent life forms. In addition to fulfilling a religious purpose, *origami* was an amusement and became increasingly popular as such among young and old alike. *Origami* is usually made from a paper rectangle or square colored and patterned to reflect the character of the object fashioned. See examples 111 and 112.

Rimpa School Term associated with artists in the sixteenth and seventeenth centuries who specialized in the reinterpretation of ancient subjects in a fresh, sometimes startling new way. Beginning with Hon'ami Kōetsu (1558–1637) and the artists who surrounded him, the Rimpa School artists produced art, craft, and calligraphy of unparalleled quality and diversity that was inspired by the classical subjects of the Heian period. The Rimpa artists produced work of a standard that had not been seen in Japan since classical times.

Shibaraku A Kabuki pose or dramatic gesture that summarizes a particular role.

Tale of Genji (Genji Monogatari) A romance of classical Japanese court life written in the Heian period by Lady Murasaki Shikibu. Considered the first novel ever written, the fifty-four chapters originally covered twenty separate scrolls with hundreds of illustrations and thousands of sheets of calligraphy. Only surviving now in fragments, *Genji* has been an inspiration as a work of art in all respects through the centuries.

Tenugui A long, rectangular piece of cloth unhemmed at the ends and decorated with woodblock print or stencil designs. Usually made of soft, absorbent cotton, *tenugui* is an all-purpose product in everyday Japanese life. Practically used as towels, these pieces of cloth are also the tightly twisted headbands worn by sushi masters and the headscarves used by women to protect their hair from the sun.

Uchiwa Round, flat, unfoldable fans, made of handmade paper *(washi)* and bamboo that are used in the summer to provide relief from the heat and in the winter to fan fires and to cool food. Decorated with simple stencil patterns, these fans are sometimes used to advertise products or business in much the same way as *bangasa*.

Ukiyo-e Literally, pictures of the floating world. Usually, these are woodblock prints or paintings with everyday or genre themes, often centered on the pursuits of pleasure and leisure—Kabuki theater, geisha, drinking, and other Edo amusements were the popular subject matter. Landscapes and works concerning natural subjects were also part of the genre. The most important artists of this school include Andō Hiroshige (1797–1858), Kitagawa Utamaro (1754–1806), and Katsushika Hokusai (1760–1849). The art from this period is one of the most enduring products of the Edo period and in many ways is responsible for our visual impressions of Japan.

Yukata An unlined cotton kimono worn by men, women, and children during the hot summer months. Usually block-printed or stenciled in blue-and-white patterns, these simple but functional garments are synonymous with summer relaxation and are usually worn at spas and in the home.

Washi Handmade Japanese paper prepared from native plants, which are harvested in the autumn, stripped of their bark, and softened with wood ash in solution. The fibers are then beaten to a pulp, formed into sheets, dried, and cut.

BIBLIOGRAPHY

Baker, Joan Stanley. *Japanese Art*.
London: Thames and Hudson, Ltd.,
1984.

Yamanaka, Norio. *The Book of Kimono*.
Tokyo: Kodansha International, 1982.

Saint-Gilles, Amaury. *Mingei: Japan's
Enduring Folk Arts*. San Francisco:
Heian International, 1982.

Herring, Ann. *The World of Chiyogami*.
Tokyo: Kodansha International, 1987.

Seattle Art Museum. *A Thousand
Cranes*. San Francisco: Chronicle
Books, 1987.